Uwe Bußmann
Silvia Schweighofer

Group Dynamics

The Nature of Groups as well as Dynamics
of Informal Groups and Dysfunctions

Anchor Compact

Bußmann, Uwe, Schweighofer, Silvia: Group Dynamics: The Nature of Groups as well
as Dynamics of Informal Groups and Dysfunctions. Hamburg, Anchor Academic
Publishing 2013
Original title of the thesis: «buchtitel»

Buch-ISBN: 978-3-95489-119-1
PDF-eBook-ISBN: 978-3-95489-619-6
Druck/Herstellung: Anchor Academic Publishing, Hamburg, 2013
Additionally: Essen, FOM – Hochschule für Oekonomie und Management, Deutschland

Bibliografische Information der Deutschen Nationalbibliothek:
Die Deutsche Nationalbibliothek verzeichnet diese Publikation in der Deutschen
Nationalbibliografie; detaillierte bibliografische Daten sind im Internet über
http://dnb.d-nb.de abrufbar

Bibliographical Information of the German National Library:
The German National Library lists this publication in the German National Bibliography.
Detailed bibliographic data can be found at: http://dnb.d-nb.de

All rights reserved. This publication may not be reproduced, stored in a retrieval system
or transmitted, in any form or by any means, electronic, mechanical, photocopying,
recording or otherwise, without the prior permission of the publishers.

Das Werk einschließlich aller seiner Teile ist urheberrechtlich geschützt. Jede Verwertung
außerhalb der Grenzen des Urheberrechtsgesetzes ist ohne Zustimmung des Verlages
unzulässig und strafbar. Dies gilt insbesondere für Vervielfältigungen, Übersetzungen,
Mikroverfilmungen und die Einspeicherung und Bearbeitung in elektronischen Systemen.

Die Wiedergabe von Gebrauchsnamen, Handelsnamen, Warenbezeichnungen usw. in
diesem Werk berechtigt auch ohne besondere Kennzeichnung nicht zu der Annahme,
dass solche Namen im Sinne der Warenzeichen- und Markenschutz-Gesetzgebung als frei
zu betrachten wären und daher von jedermann benutzt werden dürften.

Die Informationen in diesem Werk wurden mit Sorgfalt erarbeitet. Dennoch können
Fehler nicht vollständig ausgeschlossen werden und die Diplomica Verlag GmbH, die
Autoren oder Übersetzer übernehmen keine juristische Verantwortung oder irgendeine
Haftung für evtl. verbliebene fehlerhafte Angaben und deren Folgen.

Alle Rechte vorbehalten

© Anchor Academic Publishing, ein Imprint der Diplomica® Verlag GmbH
http://www.diplom.de, Hamburg 2013
Printed in Germany

Executive Summary

A group consists of some people who interact during a certain time. The number of group members is that small that there is the possibility for every member to interact with every other group member face to face. If people meet by accident who are not close friends, it will be not a group.[1]

If you want to learn more about the formation of groups you will find two leading models which display the phases of group formation. On the one hand there is the Bernstein and Lowy model on the other hand Bruce Tuckman also designed a phase model which shows the formation of groups.

Roles in groups can be positive and negative. They are supporting the group as collectivity and are not only the result of individual need, abilities and characteristics.

There are different ways for the classification of groups. Groups can be classified in general according to following characteristics:

- size
- topic / task of the group

Also a way for classifying groups is the classification according the Riemann-Thomann-Cross[2]. The next chapters this assignment shows a rough overview of the various possibilities for the classification of groups.

As there are many influencing facts for the effectiveness of groups and very contradictory interests, the advantages for one group of interest are the disadvantages for the other group of interest. The economical group of interest measures the effectiveness of a group by its productivity, flexibility and quality. The individual in a group identifies effectiveness in the group by reasonable tasks, feeling of togetherness in the group and diverse interpersonal relationships.

At workplaces, with friends together or even with complete strangers – informal groups emerge nearly everywhere in real life.

The aims of informal groups are usually – but not always – different from those of formal groups.

---

[1] Cf. Homans (1978), p. 29.

[2] A figure for visualisation of the Riemann-Thomann-Cross is shown in chapter 6.3.

The development within the group is – apart from small differences – not much different from formal groups. The process of forming, storming, norming, performing and eventually adjourning, as Professor Tuckman has described, is nearly the same. One crucial point is that informal groups are NOT part of a formal organisation and members in most of these cases are free to leave whenever they want. Therefore it is unusual to undergo e. g. a destructive storming. Before it comes to such a storming, often one or more members will leave the group in advance.

Leadership is – especially in informal groups – a difficult topic. But here again, the main characteristics of leadership are not much different from those in formal organisations.

Table of contents

Executive Summary V
Table of contents VII
List of Abbreviations X
List of Figures X
List of Tables X
1   Problem Definition 11
2   Objectives 11
3   Methodology 11
4   What is a Group about? 12
    4.1.   A Global Definition 12
    4.2.   Social groups 12
    4.3.   Other Social Gatherings – Are these also Groups? 13
5   Formation of Groups 15
    5.1.   Group Formation – The Bernstein and Lowy Model 15
        5.1.1.   Phase of Orientation 16
        5.1.2.   Phase of Power Struggle 16
        5.1.3.   Phase of Familiarity 16
        5.1.4.   Phase of Differentiation 17
        5.1.5.   Phase of Closing 17
    5.2.   Group Formation According to the Phase Model of B. Tuckman 17
    5.3.   Roles of Group Members 19
        5.3.1.   Roles in Groups According to their Function 19
        5.3.2.   Roles in Groups According to their Ranking 20
6   Types of Groups 22
    6.1.   The Size of a Group 23
    6.2.   Group Characterization According to Tasks 23
    6.3.   Group Classification as per the Riemann-Thomann-Cross 24
7   Group Effectiveness 27
    7.1.   Group Effectiveness – A Measurable Parameter? 27
    7.2.   The Size of the Group as Rating Basis for Group Effectiveness 28
    7.3.   Synergistic Effects in Groups 28
8   Implications from Research 29
9   Informal Groups – Definition 30
10   Aims of Informal Groups 31
11   Development of Informal Groups 32

11.1.		Forming (Orientation) or "All for One, One for All!"	32
	11.1.1.	Forming Process	32
	11.1.2.	Why groups form	33
11.2.		Storming (Conflict)	34
	11.2.1.	Storming Process	34
	11.2.2.	Constructive Storming	35
	11.2.3.	Destructive Storming	36
11.3.		Norming (Structure)	36
	11.3.1.	Norming Process	36
	11.3.2.	Norms	36
	11.3.3.	Roles	37
	11.3.4.	Role Conflicts	38
	11.3.5.	Intermember Relations	38
11.4.		Performing (Work)	39
	11.4.1.	Performing Process	39
	11.4.2.	Atmosphere within the Group	40
11.5.		Adjourning (Dissolution)	40
	11.5.1.	Adjourning Process	40
	11.5.2.	Planned Adjourning	40
	11.5.3.	Unplanned Adjourning	41

12 Leadership in Informal Groups 42

12.1.		What is Leadership?	42
12.2.		Specific characteristics of Leaders in Informal Groups	43
12.3.		Personal Qualities of Leaders in Groups	44
	12.3.1.	Height, Weight, Age	44
	12.3.2.	Intelligence	44
	12.3.3.	Gender	44
	12.3.4.	Personality	44
	12.3.5.	Expertise	45
	12.3.6.	Participation	45

13 Cohesion in Informal Groups 46

14 Results 47

15 Conclusion 48

16 Bibliography 49

List of Abbreviations

cf. – compare

e. g. – for example

etc. – and so forth

f – the following page

ff – the following pages

HRM – Human Resources Management

ibid. – to be found at the same place

i. e. – that is

List of Figures

Figure 1: Group formation according to Bernstein and Lowy. Source: Own interpretation. 15

Figure 2: The Reimann-Thomann-Cross used for characterization of groups. Source: According to Stahl (2002), p. 258. 25

Figure 3: Groups. Source: Own interpretation. 30

Figure 4: Tuckman-Model. Source: According to Stahl (2007). 32

Figure 5: Consensus. Source: Own interpretation. 35

Figure 6: Possible Intermember Relations. Source: Own interpretation. 39

List of Tables

Table 1: Connection of functional and ranking roles in groups. Source: Own interpretation. 22

1 Problem Definition

"Group Dynamics" is a very complex topic. There are various definitions for groups; scientific ones and non-scientific ones. In this assignment only the scientific definitions are mentioned.

A lot of scientists concern oneself with the formation, types, complexity of groups. There are a lot of different scientific views to this topic

The natures of groups as well as the specific form of informal groups are topic of these assignments.

Informal groups have nearly the same nature as formal groups. The certain differentials are realized in the second assignment with the Headline "Group Dynamics II – Dynamics of Informal Groups and Dysfunctions".

2 Objectives

The objectives of the assignments are:

- the clear scientifically definition of a group inclusive a clear dissociation from other social gatherings
- the description of group formation
- showing different types of groups
- having a closer look at the effectiveness of groups and
- a short analysis of the implications from research to groups
- a differentiation from formal and informal groups

Given that there is a specified limit for this assignment we decided to cover the above mentioned objectives in such a range that the assignment will give an overview of these.

As mentioned in the problem definition there is a wide range of scientific research to this topic. We made the effort to cover the most important scientific views and models that come up in daily life

3 Methodology

- Internet research for getting a first overview of the topic
- Reference book research
- Research in topic related learned and professional journals

- Consideration of formal/informal groups and teams that are part of our daily life

4 What is a Group about?

You will find several definitions about groups in the general literature. Here the most important points for defining a group shall be summarised.

4.1. A Global Definition

A group consists of some people who interact during a certain time. The number of group members is that small that there is the possibility for every member to interact with every other group member face to face. If people meet by accident who are not close friends, it will be not a group.[3]

This is a very general definition for groups. This definition shows the basic constituent parts of a group:

- some people
- interaction
- for a certain time

There is also a great variety of groups: families, group of pupils, groups in sports, workshop groups, working groups, ethnical and religious groups, for showing some examples. All these groups show the above mentioned three constituent parts. Recapitulating the examples for groups you come to the conclusion that some people sitting in an underground or a large number of people joining a demonstration are not a group, in the meaning of the first definition above for a group.

4.2. Social groups

Social groups are more specifically defined. The definition of social groups is based on the above mentioned three constituent parts of a group. But a social group means more. A group is a highly organised social formation that consists of a small number of members most of the time. The members are interacting individuals that are linked in an emotional and intellectual behaviour.[4]

---

[3] Cf. Homans (1978), p. 29.
[4] Cf. Battegay (1974), p. 19.

A small social group consists of three up to twenty members. Groups with more than twenty members are called big groups. That means that a couple is not a group.

Additional to the constituent parts mentioned in chapter 4.1. social groups are more detailed defined with the following parts.[5]

- rom 3 up to 20 members (for small groups) and more for large ones
- a mutual agreement upon a task or a goal
- possibility for face to face communication
- feeling of togetherness
- mutual values and standards for the interaction
- diverse social roles in a group targeting on the aim of the group

The definition for social groups shows clearly that it is important that the group members have a mutual understanding of the group and that there are some social roles in the group.

On the one hand you know now what the fundamental tees of a group are and on the other hand it is clear that a social group means more than only being more than 2 persons interacting for a certain time.

For a more concrete definition of groups let's have a look at other related terms.

4.3. Other Social Gatherings – Are these also Groups?

The audience of a football match is not a group with reference to the above mentioned definitions. There are only some people coming together with no ostensibly interest in interaction or communication. The interest of this crowd is to watch the football match. This example is valid for all major events.[6]

There must be done a differentiation to such major events from big groups. More about big groups and their specific formation you will find in chapter 6.1. of this assignment.

There are also institutions and organisations – are these forms of gatherings groups?

Social scientists speak of institution as a certain cultural and in most cases lawful, social structure. Examples for institutions can be found in our daily life: marriage, family, institutions of law

---

[5] Cf. Homans (1978), p. 16 ff.
[6] Cf. Ammon (1976), p. 92.

or economy and so on. Institutions are characterized with a social purpose and permanence, and with the making and enforcing of rules guiding cooperative human behaviour.[7]

Organisations are often parts of institutions. A common known example will explain the context of institution and organisation: The institution of education arises in the organisation form of different school types. Organisations are social system with a great formalism. It is typical of organisations that the people are only in contact to each other in a very detailed and specific manner. All parties are principally exchangeable without endangering the existence of the group itself. All these facts display that organisations are the contrary of groups. Personnel connections are not part of organisations.[8] Even organisations are conflictive to groups which have a lot of intersections and interactions. There are a lot of groups which are certainly acting inside of an organisation. The formalism of organisations impacts the acting of groups.[9]

If we think about other social gatherings which also may be groups we must not forget networks. Nowadays networking and networks are presented as important sources for communication, knowledge transfer and so on. It seems to be courteous today to have a network or to be a member of a network. There the question arises: "Are networks groups or are they part of institutions or organisations?"

Literature says that networks are more than groups but less than organisations. This means that networks consists of many social relationships of human beings or also of a group which are laxly and often informal connected.[10] Some examples for networks are insider relationships, information networks, informal supporting networks and so on.

On the one hand the definition of groups implies a certain durability and obligation of the relationship. On the other hand there are networks that underline weak relationships that are available as social resources in case of need. This determines the difference between groups and networks.[11]

After this introductory definition of groups and the dissociation from familiar social gatherings the next chapter of this assignment deals with the description of the formation of a group.

---

[7] Cf. Balzer (1993), p. 13.
[8] Cf. Nikles (2008), p. 8.
[9] Cf. Schreyögg (2003), p. 18.
[10] Cf. Lutz (2005), p. 35.
[11] Cf. Trappmann, Hummell and Sodeur (2005), p. 14.

5 Formation of Groups

If you want to learn more about the formation of groups you will find two leading models which display the phases of group formation. On the one hand there is the Bernstein and Lowy model on the other hand Bruce Tuckman also designs a phase's model which shows the formation of groups.

5.1. Group Formation – The Bernstein and Lowy Model

The formation of a group, regardless of which type of group, follows every time similar phases. Bernstein and Lowy designed the process of the formation of groups in a five phase's model. These five phases are visualized in the next figure:

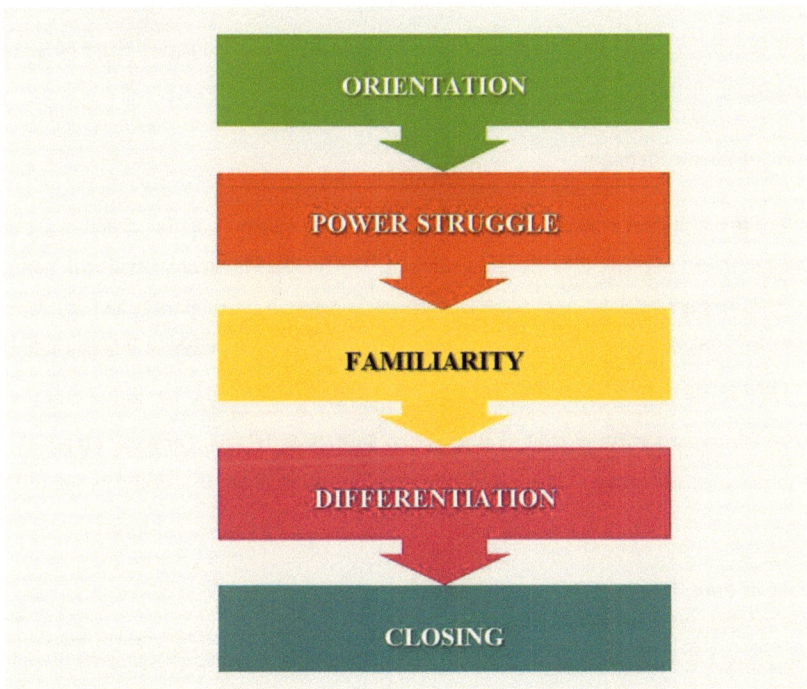

Figure 1: Group formation according to Bernstein and Lowy. Source: Own interpretation.

Bernstein and Lowy say that there are certain behaviour pattern and accruing problems in all phases of the group formation process regardless of the composition and target of a group.[12] In the following you will find a description of every phase. Every phase has its typical characteristics.

5.1.1. Phase of Orientation

In the first phase every group member is more or less uncertain. They are not familiar with the new situation. Most of the group members are rather contained, monitoring the going on in the group and focus their interest on the group leadership. Group members behaving dominantly and provokingly are refused from the other members. Every individual is interested in getting to know the other one. Becoming acquainted with each other is often for a lot of group members not very easy, they often do not know how they should act and react.[13]

Summarized we can say that the first phase of the formation process is characterized by some uncertainties of the members.

5.1.2. Phase of Power Struggle

Every member clears up him or her position in the group. Some members are interested in acting active in the group and in controlling the group actions. This process is accompanied with power struggling. This means members try to force their points and search for supporters and federates. Rivalry and competiveness are part of the interactions in the group. At this phase it is possible to some extent that group members rebel against the leadership.[14]

This phase of the group formation process is often the most essential one. For some groups it is very hard to get over this phase. Others will often return to this phase if a decision has to be made.

5.1.3. Phase of Familiarity

In this third phase the uncertainty from the first phase changes to a certain group spirit that put reliability over the members of the group. If there occur some problems the group members will speak about them in an unashamedly manner. The positions in the group are clarified. That

---

[12] Cf. Bernstein and Lowy (1973), p. 57 ff.

[13] Cf. Ibid., p. 58 ff.

[14] Cf. Ibid., p. 72 ff.

brings about that strengths and weaknesses of each member are known in the group and are accepted.[15]

Everyone uses his or her abilities to fulfil duties and tasks of the group. The group is a very important structure for every member, external interactions are rare. From an external point of view it seems that the group screens itself from its surrounding.

In this phase it is very important for the group to make decisions that influence the target achievement of the group in a very positive way.

5.1.4. Phase of Differentiation

The fourth phase is an important advancement of the third phase. The group tasks are solved further on but the interaction with external groups is more and more possible. The different abilities and originalities are mutual acceptable inputs for target-orientated solving the group tasks.[16]

5.1.5. Phase of Closing

A group will be closed if the interaction in the group is no more interesting for the members or the group tasks and targets are successfully solved. It is possible that some members are uncomfortable with the closing of the group. Furthermore it is possible that someone will be held responsible for the closing of the group.[17]

Before going into detail to the group formation process according to Mister Tuckman we have to notice here that the phases follow a scheme by no case. The phases maybe differ in their duration and in their intenseness. Furthermore it is possible that a group returns to a previous phase. This may happen in the case of having new members in the group.

5.2. Group Formation According to the Phase Model of B. Tuckman

The group formation model according to Mr. Tuckman was first shown as phase model with four steps in 1965. In 1970 he added a fifth phase to his model. The stages are called[18]:

---

[15] Cf. Bernstein and Lowy (1973), p. 76 ff.
[16] Cf. Ibid., p. 82 ff.
[17] Cf. Ibid., p. 88 ff.
[18] Cf. Stahl (2002), p. 49.

1. Forming
2. Storming
3. Norming
4. Performing
5. Adjourning

The stages of Tuckman's model begin with becoming acquainted with each other and end with the closing of the group.

It is fundamental that no single phase of the model can be omitted. Every phase is based on the previous one. The duration of the phases can be, or better are most the time very different.

Phase 1. and 2. are very important for the success of the group. In phase one we find the process of getting to know each other and seeking for certainty. The second phase consists of roll allocation. This phase may be a little bit turbulent because it is humane that persons want to act according to their individual goals. Therefore they try to find some supporters. For the leader of the group in this stage it is very important to clarify the group target and get all members on board for reaching this target.[19]

The third phase is about generating rules for the group. The development of group standards is very important for that stage. After the more or less turbulent second phase this phase of the group formation process is used to implement good manners for the interaction in the group.[20]

After generating a mutual agreed group standard the members of the group begin to act. The fourth phase is characterized by performance and target driven interaction. The members of the group are familiar with each other and they trust each other.[21]

Mr. Tuckman stopped in his first step at the fourth stage of the group formation process. But as at the beginning of this assignment mentioned a group is also characterized by a certain time limit where the group exists. And for this reason it is logical that there will also be closing phase of the group formation process. Bernstein and Lowy showed this phase for the first time in their model.

---

[19] Cf. Stahl (2002), p. 67 and 95-96.
[20] Cf. Ibid., p. 127-129.
[21] Cf. Ibid., p. 153.

The fifth and at the same time the last phase of the Tuckman model is called "adjourning stage". In this phase the group will be closed. The target of the group is more or less fulfilled and the members will be ready for new tasks.[22]

This was a rough description of the Tuckman model. It shows even the stages are different named, a lot of similarities to the Bernstein and Lowy model. In both models the group members play different roles. Therefore let's have a closer look at the different roles members of a group have.

5.3. Roles of Group Members

Roles in groups can be positive and negative. They are supporting the group as collectivity and are not only the result of individual need, abilities and characteristics.

5.3.1. Roles in Groups According to their Function

In the related literature you will find three types of roles in general according to their function in the group. They are all a result of monitoring and analysing groups[23]:

1. task roles
2. sustainment and system roles
3. negative roles

There are also some models known that are based on characteristic and personality typology. There is a great difference between such personality psychological typologies and the social-psychological-group dynamic views. The first mentioned one assumes that all group members implement their own personality into the group and define according to their personality their role in the group. The group dynamic view assumes on the contrary that roles will be formed by the tasks in the group and the personal formation of the group. This implies that the roles in the group are only partly formed by the individual personalities. According to this a group is only working when there are a certain number of roles in the group.[24]

Let's have a closer look at the three types of roles mentioned before in groups according to their function.

---

[22] Cf. Mills (1976), p. 88.
[23] Cf. Antons (2000), p. 226 ff.
[24] Cf. Edding and Schattenhofer (2009), p. 424.

Task roles are characterized by initiative and action. Group members who play that role are searching for information and different views but they also put forward opinions and publish information. Group members who have a task role are responsible for generating tasks, for coordinating them and for summarizing them.[25]

Sustainment and system roles are important for the group because members who play this role are responsible for motivation and encouragement. They observe the group rules and express the feeling of belonging together. Group members who play a sustainment and system role avoid friction by arbitrating between the other group members.[26]

Negative roles are also part of almost every group, but it is the task of the group leader to control them and to restrain them. Group members who play the negative role in the group display aggressive behaviour that block respectively foil the group development. This role is characterized by the following bad manners of behaviour: searching for adherence, rivalling among each other and also baking out of the group.[27]

5.3.2. Roles in Groups According to their Ranking

The ranking in groups is based upon the need that a group must be lead, coordinated, decisions must be made, and the decisions and or views of the group must be forwarded to other people outside the group. That is the first motive for having a ranking inside groups.[28]

The second motive is that individuals are used to have rankings. A ranking in the group provides a basis for the requirement of differentiation of the group members who pursuit career possibilities within the group. When you observe animals, you will find rankings in almost every species.[29]

Now let's have a closer look on the ranking roles in groups of humans. We will find in almost every group the following group members, playing one of these roles[30]:

- the leader,
- the favourite,

---

[25] Cf. Barker, Wahlers, Cegala and Kibler (1983), p. 63 f.
[26] Cf. Däumling, Fengler, Nellessen and Svenssson (1974), p. 144.
[27] Cf. Battegay (1974), p. 61.
[28] Cf. Kretschmar (1994), p. 14.
[29] Cf. Ibid., p. 15.
[30] Cf. Langmaack and Braune-Krickau (2000), p. 139 ff.

- the brave,
- the follower,
- the opponent,
- the scapegoat and
- the outsider

The leader of a group is responsible for coordination and cohesion of the group. The leader leads the other group members according to reach the group target. Are there no formal leader members who are playing the role of the brave or favourite go for the role as a leader. Both roles are not compatible[31].

The role of the favourite is responsible for keeping the group together. He or she personifies the emotional part of the needs in the group. As mentioned above, the favourite is not able to lead the group. This role has not enough power to personify the target of the group. Instructions of the favourite are often not complied by the other members.[32]

The brave represents the normative goals of the group. Therefore this role cannot be the favourite of the group members.[33]

The follower orientates his action according to the leader of the group. Followers can be easily guided and directed by the group leader.[34]

The opponent is a strong group member with leading qualities. He or she has therefore a good relation to the group leader but is not the leader of the group. Because of this fact the opponent often disputes the leader conscious or unconscious. The role is also responsible for bringing social conflicts forward.[35]

The member of the group who plays the role of the scapegoat is often the weakest one. This role is often hold responsible for failing in reaching the group's targets. The reason for not reaching a goal in the group is in this context often social not wanted to come to light.[36]

---

[31] Cf. Homans (1978), p. 56.

[32] Cf. Runde and Warmbrunn (2006), p. 40.

[33] Cf. Ibid., p. 45.

[34] Cf. Runde and Warmbrunn (2006), p. 43.

[35] Cf. Reeves (1970), p. 286 f.

[36] Cf. Runde and Warmbrunn (2006), p. 44.

The outsider has often the function of a "clown". In some few cases it maybe that the outsider is a consultant of the group.[37]

If we connect the function orientated roles with the roles according to the ranking in the group we will find out that there are more ranking related roles as task roles than other ones. For this just have a look at the following table:

Table 1: Connection of functional and ranking roles in groups. Source: Own interpretation.

Roles according to Functions	Roles according to Rankings
Task roles	Favourite
	Brave
	Follower
Sustainment and System Roles	Scapegoat
	Leader
Negative Roles	Outsider
	Opponent

The table shows clearly that only one can be the leader and that it is important that only few members are playing negative roles in the group. The major members are playing task roles that will support the process for reaching the target of the group.

In this chapter of the assignment you have learned about roles that are played by members in the group. The next chapter is about the different types of groups with its diverse aims.

6 Types of Groups

Everybody is some times in his or her life member of a group. There are different roles which can be played by the group members we learned this in the chapter before. Now let's find a systematic for characterizing the various types of groups.

There are different ways for the classification of groups. Groups can be classified in general according to following characteristics:

- size
- topic / task of the group

---

[37] Cf. Reeves (1970), p. 321.

Another way for classifying groups is the classification according to the Riemann-Thomann-Cross.[38] The next chapters of this assignment show a rough overview of the various possibilities for the classification of groups.

6.1. The Size of a Group

If we rank groups corresponding to their size we will have small groups on the one hand and big groups on the other hand. This is such a simple classification. The dissociation of a group, whether small or big, to the mass is shown in chapter 4.3. of this assignment.

Small groups are specified in general in chapter 4.2. of this assignment. The members of small groups must be able to do additional structural work in the group. Members who feel only responsible for tasks in the group with regard to the content are often a problem in small groups. Small groups demand flexibility and multi tasking of their members.[39]

Big groups are more likely to be better organized as small groups. Members of big groups play more or less clear roles. Task and system roles are clearly defined. The leader of a big group claims to support a strong company in the group, to allocate the tasks and to organize the process to reach the aim of the group.[40]

6.2. Group Characterization According to Tasks

The classification, according to the topics and/or the tasks shows a great variety. Here there are some examples with no claim to be complete: rehabilitation and self-awareness groups, self-aiding groups, working teams, compelled groups like classes in school and some more.[41]

Rehabilitation, self-aiding and similar groups are specially compounded and have a certain task. These groups are not topic in this assignment but should be named for having an overview of the variety of groups. In working life we turn up more or less often in working teams. Therefore we will specify this "group" a little bit more detailed.

Not every group is a team but every team is a group. The term team is a collective term for working and tasks related groups. Team members have to cooperate to reach the team aim. In

---

[38] A figure for visualisation of the Riemann-Thomann-Cross is shown in chapter 6.3.
[39] Stahl (2002), p. 87 ff.
[40] Cf. Seliger (2008), p. 38.
[41] Cf. Mann (1999), p. 65.

some ones working life you will find teams for a certain specified period.[42] Teams have two "meanings". On the one hand they are formed for reaching a working aim, on the other hand they are also social systems. Teamwork is therefore a challenging form of cooperation.[43]

Working teams are daily business in a lot companies. Teamwork is used in companies and organisations to connect productivity and humanization of the work.

Another possibility to classify groups will be shown in the next chapter.

6.3. Group Classification as per the Riemann-Thomann-Cross

The Riemann-Thomann-Cross shows two dimensions. On the one hand the distinguishing dimensions (closeness/distance) and on the other hand the predictability (duration/change).[44]

If we use the Riemann-Thomann-Cross for classifying groups according communication specific notes we will have four different types of groups. The figure below shows these four categories of groups:

---

[42] Cf. Sader (1998), p. 39 f.
[43] Cf. Gellert and Nowak (2004), p. 59 ff.
[44] Stahl (2002), p. 252.

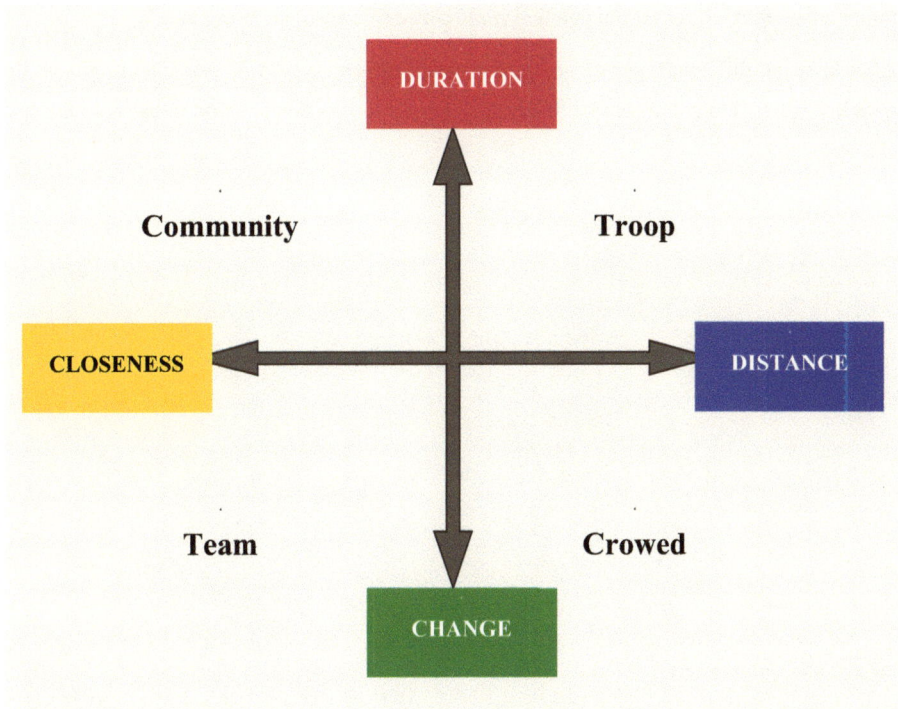

Figure 2: The Reimann-Thomann-Cross used for characterization of groups. Source: According to Stahl (2002), p. 258.

Members of groups shown in the dimension of closeness have a certain feeling of togetherness. Their place for desires and emotions. The aim of the group is the success of the group. The groups in the dimension of distance are accompanied by the groups in the dimension of closeness. In this dimension the members of groups are acting factually, emotions are not welcome. The success of the individual is in the foreground. Groups that are founded for certain duration are well planned and are based on a specific schedule and on specific norms. The contrary we will find in the dimension of change. Improvisation, breaking rules and short-term decisions are significant for groups that are every time in change[45].

All four dimensions and their placed groups show different qualities. The group members show different behavioural pattern that support the group. The community is affected by closeness and duration. Teams are also in the dimension of closeness but their working together is affected by

---

[45] Cf. Stahl (2002), p. 257.

change. Troops and crowds are both groups that are defined in the dimension of distance. But troops are established for certain duration while crowds are changing every time[46].

After knowing different types of groups and members who play different roles in groups the question arises: "Do groups work effectively?" For answering this question please read the next chapter.

---

[46] Cf. Ibid., p. 258.

7 Group Effectiveness

Before we go into detail, let's raise some questions to the title of this chapter:

1. Do groups work effectively?
2. Which influencing factors have to be known for controlling the effectiveness of groups?
3. Is it possible to enhance group effectiveness?

7.1. Group Effectiveness – A Measurable Parameter?

At first glance it seems to be rather an economical than a social psychological question of group effectiveness. This is supported by the fact that groups are formed for having economic or social success. When groups are not effective any longer they begin to break up or split up and are organized to bigger upper-level groupings. This is the fact for self-organized groups. Groups with only economical purpose run the risk of being broken up, being displaced or being taken over by competitors when the group shows a lack of effectiveness. A lack of effectiveness in social and economic groups results in the general risk of being broken up. The effectiveness in groups is therefore a very important topic, which depends on different quantitatively and qualitatively influencing factors, the structure of the group and the processes inside the group[47].

Output orientated effectiveness can be easily measured. The qualitative effects of group goals with social background like motivation, self-fulfilment and so on are often only verbally describable. For the valuation of the group effectiveness it is common to compare the result of the group with the results of an individual person or of parallel acting individuals without any further interaction[48].

As there are many influencing facts for the effectiveness of groups and very contradictory interests, the advantages for one group of interest are the disadvantages for the other group of interest. The economical group of interest measures the effectiveness of a group by its productivity, flexibility and quality. The individual in a group identifies effectiveness in the group by reasonable tasks, feeling of togetherness inside the group and diverse interpersonal relationships. If groups are only matched with clear quantitative economic facts the profitability will be a

---

[47] Cf. Edding and Schattenhofer (2009), p. 128 ff.
[48] Cf. Reeves (1970), p. 331 f.

possible yardstick. This method is not possible for matching qualitative facts. Therefore we have to distinguish between quantitative and qualitative effectiveness.[49]

7.2. The Size of the Group as Rating Basis for Group Effectiveness

As shown in the previous chapters of this assignment, groups may be classified by the size. Just to remember, there are small groups, teams and big groups.

As the success of a group depends on clear formulated target agreements we can say that the size of the group has a great influence on the effectiveness. Target agreements are more effective in small groups than in big groups. With increasing group size the possibility increases as well that there is a lack of motivation and coordination. Such lacks in the process may cause a negative influence on reaching the group aims and in general on the group performance. Communication and coordination processes are more functional in small groups than in big ones. This positively affects the effectiveness of groups.[50]

7.3. Synergistic Effects in Groups

Synergy is determined in general as coactions in the meaning of mutual support. In connection with group effectiveness it means that "the group is greater than the sum of its individual members that groups are formed of – to achieve goals that could be reached by unilateral activity."[51] We can also say that synergy is the heart of effectiveness in a group but synergy is not alone accountable for effectiveness[52].

---

[49] Cf. Edding and Schattenhofer (2009), p. 132 ff.
[50] Cf. Reeves (1970), p. 333.
[51] Reeves (1970), p. 334.
[52] Cf. Reeves (1970), p. 335.

8 Implications from Research

As the bibliography of this assignment shows you can find literature that is published on the topic group dynamics and on familiar topics twenty and more years ago. The formation of individuals into groups, is an important topic for psychologists and sociologists. Working groups and teams become more and more a concern in times of increasing productivity and industrialization for the economists in the thirties. Researchers in working and organisations psychology developed the model of the "social man" which claims that human beings are defining their identity also by the relationships with other individuals. The social surrounding of the individual became also more and more important in therapeutic interventions. Therefore Moreno implemented in the twenties and thirties of the last century the psychodrama as a first form of the group therapy.[53]

The original theoretical context to which a lot of researchers correspond to is the field theory of Lewin. Lewin assumed that personal and surrounding characteristics are a function for behaviour. Human beings and the surrounding are mutual independent in his theory.[54]

The field theoretical considerations of Lewin were no theories which could be used for exact predictions for empirical research. With these theories a description of the behaviour of individuals is not possible. It is only possible to reconstruct them. Nevertheless the heuristics have made a lot of scientists research in the field as well as in the laboratory on this topic.

---

[53] Cf. Edding and Schattenhofer (2009), p. 51 ff.

[54] Cf. Lewin (1936), in Arnscheid (1999), p. 20.

9 Informal Groups – Definition

As mentioned in Part I – The Nature of Groups – there are two different types of groups:

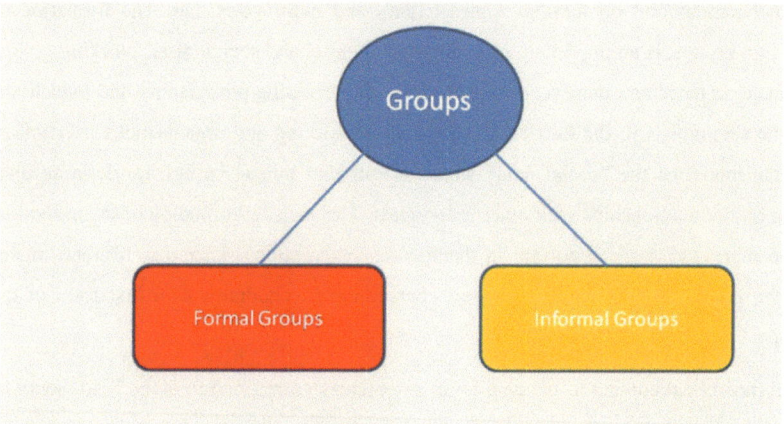

Figure 3: Groups. Source: Own interpretation.

This part of the assignment focuses – despite great similarities – on informal groups only.

If people have a common aim, these people can gather spontaneous by groups. The informal group in an organization is the interlocking social structure that determines how people work together[55] in practice.

It is the aggregate of behaviour, interactions, norms, personal and professional connections through which work gets done and relationships are built among people who share a common organizational affiliation or cluster of affiliations.

In practice people often assemble in informal groups if they have the same interests, come from the same ethnic background or if they are friends.

Every group which is NOT part of a formal organization is called an informal group.[56]

---

[55] In this context the phrase „work together" refers to the workplace as well as to activities in leisure time.
[56] Cf. Kretschmar (1994), p. 33 f.

10 Aims of Informal Groups

Especially in informal groups, the aims can be very different. This type of group sometimes is only formed for one purpose and diverges after a short period of time.

Therefore there are no "typical" aims which are pursued by informal groups.

The aims are often a result of where and by which coincidence the groups have assembled. E. g.: Groups can form themselves at the workplace or the fitness centre with completely different objectives.

At work, a common aim can be the improvement of the working conditions or to achieve a rise in salary. In a fitness centre it is possible that the members amalgamate to reach an extension off the opening hours. For these aims smaller or bigger groups can assemble.

Often, but not always, after the achievement of the common goal, the group splits up. In some cases the group stays together to achieve another, different goal. This objective is not necessarily connected to the first aim achieved previously by the informal group.

E. g.: After the successfully achievement of the extension of the opening hours of the fitness centre, now the same group pursues the redecoration of the locker room.

11 Development of Informal Groups

As the retired Professor Tuckman[57] has defined, there are five stages of group development:

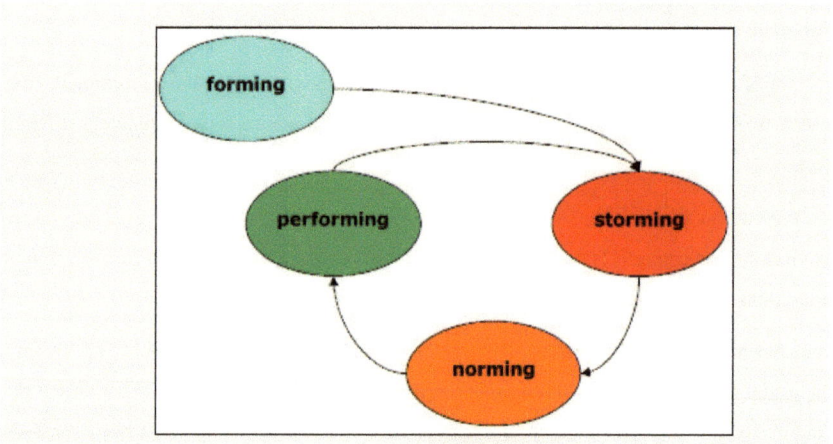

Figure 4: Tuckman-Model. Source: According to Stahl (2007).

The stages in group dynamic in informal groups are not different from formal groups. However, some points have a different characteristic in either type of group.

11.1. Forming (Orientation) or "All for One, One for All!"
11.1.1. Forming Process

The forming process is a situation of uncertainty with a lack of rules, which have to be developed virtually out of nothing.[58]

In formal groups a minimum of two conditions is needed:

1. A basically self-concept and a connected expectation of the official aim of the cooperation – "To which aim do we get together?"

2. and therefore an imagination of the adequate form of the cooperation –

    "Due to these aims, in what way should we work together?"[59]

---

[57] Bruce Wayne Tuckman, American Psychologist (born 1938).

[58] Cf. Stahl (2007), p. 64.

[59] Cf. Stahl (2007), p. 64 f.

In informal groups in majority of cases also both conditions exist, but in some exceptions only the first is essential.

Sometimes informal groups band together instantly without further consideration. Therefore the second condition is negligible.

11.1.2. Why groups form

There are several different thinkable ways how informal groups can come together. E. g.:

- They are friends
- They share the same interests
- They are stuck in the same situation
- They derive from the same ethnic group
- They do the same job etc.

Friends often form groups without thinking about it. As condition one says, only a common aim is needed. Therefore even a number of people which come together for a game of cards are an informal group. Some friends who meet every Saturday for a motorbike tour also have formed an informal group.

But people don't even have to be friends to form this kind of group! E.g.: A group of joggers who run around a lake together every Sunday morning have – without knowing – formed an informal group. These people often don't know each other. The just have the same interest: jogging.

Sometimes people are stuck in the same situation. E. g.: A number of people – completely unknown to each other – have been informed, that the expected flight to Munich has been cancelled due to the weather conditions. These people start to discuss about different ways of transportation and how to response to the airline. These people pursue a common aim, they have formed an informal group.

If citizen belong to the same ethnic group, the often have the same problems and concerns. Due to that, the form groups with no officially installed leader[60] to achieve their aims.

---

[60] For information about leadership in informal groups, please see chapter 12.

The workplace is also quite often a place where informal groups are formed.

In all companies there exists – next to the formal organization – an informal organization as well.[61] The informal group is a special part of the informal organization.[62]

These groups may just come together during lunch breaks to share company-related information, or to pursue actively "hard" objectives such as an improvement of food quality in the canteen. Often these groups are created independently by colleagues regardless of position, the actual job in the organization or age.

For every manger it is essential to know the informal groups and the informal leaders in his (or her) area of responsibility. Thereby the manager can benefit from the activity of the informal group in order to lead the formal organization (i. e. the company itself).

11.2. Storming (Conflict)
11.2.1. Storming Process

Storming is the phase were conflicts of objectives are clarified.[63]

After the forming process, the group gives – to a certain degree – safety to its members. The "aim" – to be part of the group – is achieved by all persons involved.

The next step is a far-reaching differentiation of the group interior which lets differences emerge even clearer.[64]

In informal groups, where every member is a member by his own will, members want to express themselves to achieve their personal aims.

Imagine an informal group of poker buddies which comes together every Friday night. In this group one of the buddies is responsible for the money, but another member distrusts this man and wants to administer the money himself. This leads undoubtedly to a conflict.

People are different by nature. Therefore different people have different ideas and different needs. Sometimes this leads to smaller misunderstandings, sometimes to bigger ones. This depends on the unequal personal objectives of the individuals.

---

[61] Cf. Kretschmar (1994), p. 19.
[62] Cf. Ibid., p. 29 ff.
[63] Cf. Stahl (2007), p. 92.
[64] Cf. Stahl (2007), p. 92.

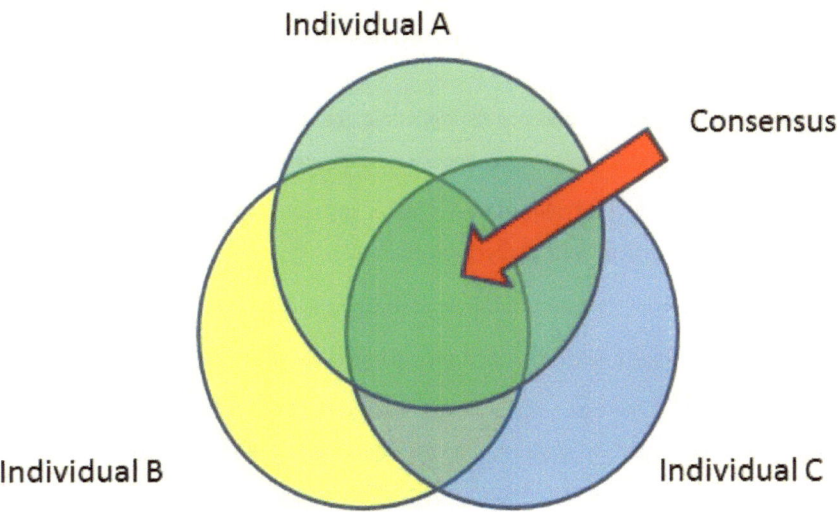

Figure 5: Consensus. Source: Own interpretation.

It is important in every group to find a consensus which is acceptable for everyone within the group.

Is this not possible – through the lack of a formal structure – often a single member or a small group of members leave the group. Or – even worse – the group splits up completely.

Through dissociation and dispute the group members can be noticed as individuals. The dispute helps the members to clarify their own aims.[65]

11.2.2. Constructive Storming

A constructive storming can be distinguished from a destructive storming by a mutual understanding and the chance for every participant to express his or her opinion freely. During a constructive storming it is not important who is right or who tells the truth, but that everyone treats the others with respect.

This kind of storming is the only one which can be used in informal groups. Many people do not want to face a storming which does not stick not to these ideas and prefer to leave an informal group before it comes to a destructive storming.

---

[65] Ibid., p. 100.

11.2.3. Destructive Storming

A constructive storming has to happen at the right time, the right place, with the right subject. Is that not possible, the threat to slide in a destructive storming even bigger.

In this kind of storming, the real subjects do not matter anymore. The discussion focuses in most of the cases on proxy subjects (i. e. "Stellvertreterthemen").

This often leads to an even more heated dispute in which no suitable goal can be reached.

In these cases the storming has to be stopped and continued under new conditions.

Fortunately, in most of the cases, the storming is successful and a concord can be reached. Without this consensus, the next stage in group development can never be reached.

11.3. Norming (Structure)
11.3.1. Norming Process

In the phase of norming the "rules of engagement" for the group become established.[66]

Each group is unique in many ways, but beneath the surface there are certain structures that are common to virtually all groups. All but the most ephemeral groups develop structure:

Norms, roles, and intermember relations.[67]

11.3.2. Norms

Groups sometimes write down and formally adopt norms. This is not limited to formal groups, sometimes informal groups write down their rules, too.

E. g.: Roles for a card game. The members of the group have to obey these particular norms.

But in most informal groups norms are not written down. These norms develop from meetings of the members. Often the norms are not even spoken out. Everybody in the group knows them, because of common-sense. E. g.: Friends planning a surprise party. It is clear to everyone that is it forbidden to talk about it outside of the particular group.

---

[66] Cf. Stahl (2007), p. 127.
[67] Cf. Forsyth (1999), p. 119.

11.3.3. Roles

Even informal groups have certain role allocation (i. e. "Rollenverteilung"). Group behaviour is not random behaviour. Studies of group development quickly reveal patterns.[68]

These roles are divided in

- Role differentiation
- Task roles
- Socioemotional roles

Role differentiation is the development of distinct roles in a group, such as:

- Leader
- Follower or
- Complainer

Task role means the position in a group occupied by group members who perform goal-oriented, task-focused behaviours. E. g.:

- Initiator/contributor
- Opinion seeker
- Information giver
- Etc.

Socioemotional roles are positions in a group filled by members who perform supportive, interpersonally accommodative behaviours. E. g.:

- Encourager
- Harmonizer
- Compromiser
- Etc.[69] [70]

---

68 Cf. Luft (1984), p. 21.

[69] Cf. Forsyth (1999), p. 120 ff.

[70] For more examples of roles in groups see: Forsyth (1999), p. 127.

These roles in a group emerge from pure behaviour, they are usually not assigned.

Sometimes a group decides to enhance its efficiency by organization and decides to elect a leader or other persons with specific functions within the group. As a result of that the group develops a formal structure and is no informal group any more.

11.3.4. Role Conflicts

In all groups, conflicts can arise. The reasons are often the discrepancies between the natural behaviour of a member and the way somebody is expected to behave. A person's personality, for example, matches not necessarily with the way of being a leader. The way a certain group member is expected to tackle a task can cause irritation, tension, anger or even withdrawal or other possible reactions, if the way this member works is much different from expectations.[71] All groups face the problem of fitting particular roles with certain persons. Self-imposed constrains may interfere with the disclosure of role-based problems. Some members may simply express boredom, others – due to the lack of restrictions in informal groups – just withdraw.

Every conflict, if this conflict is carried out in a constructive way, is also an opportunity to strengthen the group as a whole as mentioned in the previous chapter.

11.3.5. Intermember Relations

In all kind of groups, the members develop a certain structure of the relations among each other.

These stable variations in dominance, prestige and control among the group members reflect the group's status relations, or authority relations. Status patterns are often hierarchical and centralized.[72]

Even in small groups there is always a leader and often this leader has a deputy who acts for him. Imagine a loose group of cyclists who meet once a month for a 100 km tour. Somebody has to plan the route, this usually is the leader. If the leader is unable to attend the appointment, somebody else has to plan the route. Without talking about it, always the same person plans the route instead. This is the group's deputy.

---

[71] Sabrin & Jones (1955) in Luft (1984), p. 21.

[72] Cf. Forsyth (1999), p. 131.

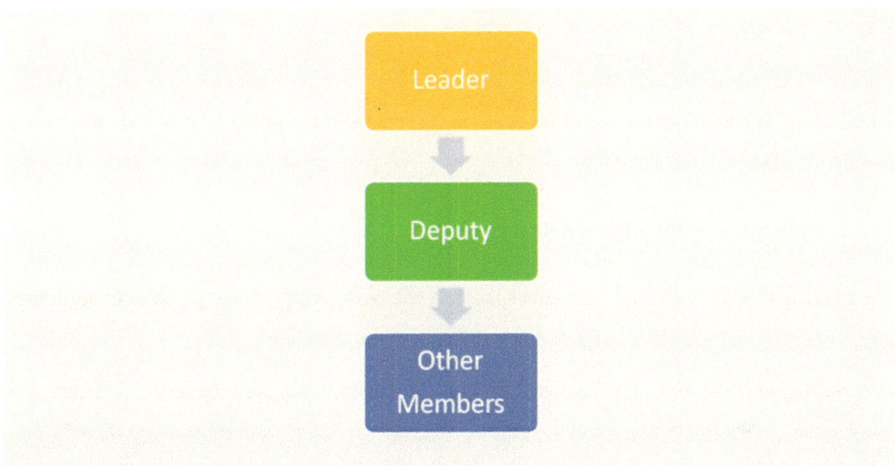

Figure 6: Possible Intermember Relations. Source: Own interpretation.

In bigger and more complex groups, there can be a structure which is even more complex and multi-layered.

11.4. Performing (Work)
11.4.1. Performing Process

This phase is distinguished literally by the work in which the intermember cooperation derived from the "rules of engagement" and the structure of cooperation can be seen.[73]

Not all groups reach this stage, characterized by a state of interdependence and flexibility. Some groups collapse before it comes to the specific working phase.

Now everyone knows each other well enough to be able to work together and to trust each other enough to allow independent activity. Roles and responsibilities change according to the need in an almost seamless way. This stage in group-dynamic is the stage where the group eventually is able to pursue its common aim, the reason why the group has established.

Nobody should underestimate the power of informal groups. These groups can have a powerful influence on the effectiveness of an organization (e. g. Company) and can even subvert its formal goals. But the informal group's role is not limited to resistance. The impact of the informal group upon the even larger formal group depends on the norms that the informal group sets.[74] So the

---

[73] Cf. Stahl (2007), p. 154.

[74] See Cap. 11.3.

informal group can make the formal organization more effective, too. This stage is the perfect stage for the solution of all kinds of problems the group wants to tackle.

Finally in this phase the individual can experience if he or she is "right or wrong" in this particular group. Every member can see if his/her strength can help the group or if his/her weaknesses hamper the group.

11.4.2. Atmosphere within the Group

If complications do not occur, the atmosphere in the performing of the group is concentrated, target-oriented and a sense of responsibility arises in every member.

It is functional if the aims are functional and personal if the aims are interpersonal. There is no manipulative complexity of the low – or high context (i. e. "Sach – und Beziehungsebene").[75]

If intergroup-complications occur, it is time for reforming the group.

11.5. Adjourning (Dissolution)
11.5.1. Adjourning Process

Ten years after first describing the four stages, Professor Tuckman revisited his original work and described this final stage. Some authors describe this stage actually as "Deforming and Mourning".

There are two types of adjourning:

11.5.2. Planned Adjourning

The planned adjourning is usually the ending of the group through reaching the intended goal. This adjourning is sometimes also mentioned as a "Successful Adjourning". E. g.: An informal group of neighbours had pursued the objective of getting a new playground for children in their suburb. Finally this petition was conceded by the cognizant municipality.

After the aim of the group is reached, the group in its present combination is not needed any more.

This is a pleasant situation for the former group members. Nevertheless, this can be – as the alternative title "Deforming and Mourning" suggests – also an unhappy stage.

---

[75] Cf. Stahl (2007), p. 166 f.

Over the collective work together in the group, personal bonds have strengthened, new friendships have possibly emerged. Now, at the end of the common objective, team members think retrospectively of the elapsed time with melancholy. Despite the joyful feeling of an achieved aim, some members would like to continue with the group not for reaching a (new) aim, but for the individual friendship.

11.5.3. Unplanned Adjourning

From time to time unplanned adjourning occurs as well.

3.5.3.1 Internal Unplanned Adjourning

It means that the reason for the splitting of the group comes from the group itself.

This can be:

- Leaving of an important group member
- Insolvable problems in the group
- Lack of interest in the pursued aim
- Etc.

Every group has so called "key-persons" in. These are not necessarily the (informal) leaders of the group, but often people who have important duties or responsibilities within the group. E. g.: The cashier in a group of card-players. If one of these people leaves the group, often members question the group and it aims in whole. The reasons for leaving the group can be multiple. E. g.: Dissatisfaction with other group members or the aims of the group or a relocation to another city far away or just the lack of time.

Common reasons for an unplanned adjourning are internal problems between the members which cannot be solved. Especially in informal groups people feel not obliged to stay in the group if greater problems occur. They just leave the group. Thus the group collapses.

Sometimes, often during a longer period of time, people lose the interest in the goal, once pursued. If group members have altered their objectives or do not see the outcome of the group, they just leave the group. This, again, can result in splitting-up of the group.

These problems occur more often in informal than in formal groups. In informal groups the members are free to leave the group whenever they want. In formal organizations – especially in formal groups at work – it is not that easy, sometimes even impossible to leave the group.

3.5.3.2 External Unplanned Adjourning

- The indented aim is all in all not needed any more
- The intended aim has already been reached by other groups or through other means
- Alternation of the initial situation (the aim is not needed any more)
- Alternation of the initial situation (it makes no sense to pursue the aim any more)
- Etc.

If the intended aim is not needed any more, it makes no sense to pursue it any more, therefore the group can adjourn. If the aim of a particular group is reached by another group before the first group has reached it, again it makes no sense to operate the group any further. Due to that the group can split-up.

A group, in particular an informal group, is usually launched out of a certain situation. If these situation changes, sometimes the aim is not necessary any more. E. g.: There is no children's playground in a particular neighbourhood. A group of neighbours wants to collect money to build a new playground. A lot of money is needed, this takes time. In the meantime all the children in this neighbourhood have grown up and are now too old to play in a playground. This alternation has made the aim obsolete.

Another possibility would be that the city council itself builds a new playground just two streets away. In this case, the initial goal, to collect money for a playground, is senseless.

12   Leadership in Informal Groups

12.1. What is Leadership?

Leaders are as universal as the groups they lead, but their ubiquity has not robbed their mystery. If you ask, "What would you change to turn an inept group into a productive one?" most people would answer, "the leader".[76]

So, what is a leader ... and even more interesting: What is a good leader? Especially in informal groups the leader is not assigned through strict rules but comes out of the equal group members by the formation of the group.

A leader must not be assigned or elected in most of the informal groups. The leader is the person which makes decisions to bring the group forward.

---

[76] Forsyth (1999), p. 339.

As complicated as the question: "What is a good leader?", is the question: "What are the characteristics of a good leader?"

Here are some quotations of famous people who tried to explain good leadership:[77]

Harry S. Truman: *"A leader is a man who has the ability to get other people to do what they don't want to do, and like it."*

Ho Chi Min: *"To use people is like using wood. A skilled worker can make use of all kinds of wood, whether it is big or small, straight or curved."*

Lao Tzu: *"A leader is best when people barely know that he exists, not so good when people acclaim him, worst when they despise him."*

The political scientist James McGregor Burns asserts in 1978 that leadership is "one of the most observed and least understood phenomena on earth."

12.2. Specific characteristics of Leaders in Informal Groups

Many of the characteristics of leaders in informal groups are similar to those of formal organizations, others are unique. One attribute of informal groups is rotational leadership. In some groups this is used excessively, in others never. Formal groups have very seldom a rotational leadership.

The informal leader emerges as the individual possessing qualities that the other members perceive as helpful to the satisfaction of their specific needs at the moment; as the needs change so does the leader. Only rarely does a single individual possess all of the leadership characteristics needed to fill the various needs of the group.

Unlike the formally appointed leader who has a defined position by which he can influence others, the informal leader does not possess formal power. If the informal leader fails to meet the group's expectations, he or she is often deposed and replaced by another. The informal group's judgment of its leaders tends to be quicker and more cold-blooded than that of most formal groups.[78]

---

[77] Ibid., p. 341.

[78] Cf. Accel (2009).

12.3. Personal Qualities of Leaders in Groups[79]
12.3.1. Height, Weight, Age

Leaders often differ physically from the other group members. They are often older, taller and heavier than average group members. Ralph Stogdill[80] found, that there is a certain correlation between height and leadership and a link between age and leadership. But in informal groups this link is not always prominent, however in formal organizations, the leader is often older than the subordinates.

12.3.2. Intelligence

Stogdill also discovered a link between intellectual ability and leadership, but the average correlation is a small one. Groups appear to prefer leaders who are more intelligent, although the discrepancy cannot be too big, otherwise it leads to problems in communication, trust and social sensitivity.

12.3.3. Gender

In formal groups, mostly men are the leaders. In Germany only 30 % of executive positions are occupied by women.[81]

This is not different in informal groups. A lone man in an otherwise all-female group often becomes the leader, whereas the lone woman in an otherwise all-male group has little influence.[82]

12.3.4. Personality

Early leadership-researchers believed that leaders possess certain personality treats that set them apart from others. In the nineteen-fifties this view was rejected. Founded on hundreds studies, several reviewers concluded that there is only a small correlation between personality traits and leadership.[83]

---

[79] Cf. Forsyth (1999), p. 348 ff.
[80] American Psychologist (1904-1978).
[81] Cf. Deutsches Institut für Wirtschaftsforschung (2006).
[82] Cf. Crocker and McGraw (1984) in Forsyth (1999), p. 349 f.
[83] Cf. Mann (1959) and Stogdill (1948) in Forsyth (1999), p. 350.

Nowadays this rejection seems to be premature. Researchers developed the so-called "big five dimensions of leadership" which are identified by dozens of different scientists:

- *extraversion:* outgoing, sociable, interpersonal, expressive, gregarious
- *agreeableness:* friendly, warm, likable, generous, kind
- *conscientiousness:* responsible, achievement, oriented, dependable, self-controlled
- *stability:* emotional controlled, assured, not anxious, balanced
- *intelligence:* intellectually able, open to new ideas and experiences, cultured

Good leaders have high scores in all five of these dimensions as numbers of studies have revealed.[84]

12.3.5. Expertise

When groups work collectively on tasks, individuals with more expertise usually rise higher in leadership hierarchy. Groups are more willing to follow and take directions from people who have demonstrated their ability in former tasks than incompetent persons.[85] Low skills seem to be an even stronger factor to exclude group members from leadership.[86] E. g.: In a soccer squat of friends (i. e. "Thekenmannschaft") nobody would elect the worst player to become the trainer of the team.

12.3.6. Participation

Participation is one of the key figures of leadership. People who often talk in a group are more likely to become the leader than other which does not talk that much.[87] Even more interesting: It does not matter what a person says (the so-called "babble effect")! People who make several but useless remarks are more likely to become a leader than people who make fewer remarks. Quantity clearly overpowers quality.[88] Other group members account somebody who is highly involved in a discussion as a person which is highly interested in the group and willing to take

---

[84] Cf. Barrick & Mount (1994) and Hoagan et al. (1994) and Kirkpatrick & Locke (1991) and Ones, Mount, Barrick & Hunter in Forsyth (1999), p. 351.

[85] Cf. Goldmann & Fraas (1965) and Hollander (1965) in Forsyth (1999), p. 352.

[86] Cf. Palmer (1962) in Forsyth (1999), p. 352.

[87] Cf. Burke (1974) and Stein & Heller (1979, 1983) in Forsyth (1999), p. 352.

[88] Cf. Sorrentino & Boutillier (1975) in Forsyth (1999), p. 352.

responsibility for its forthcoming. People with fewer rates in participation are regarded as not, or less interested in the group and their problems.

13   Cohesion in Informal Groups

Groups, like all living things, develop in the course of time. The group may begin as a collection of strangers, but before long, uncertainty gives way to conflict, which in turn gives way to cohesion, as members become bound to their group by strong social bonds.[89]

Definition:

The term "cohesiveness" has been defined as "the resultant of forces which are acting on the members to stay in the group".[90]

Everybody knows the difference between cohesive group and groups that are not cohesive – cohesive groups are unified.

But cohesion is the force, which binds the group together! Without cohesion there is no or less unity in the group.

Groups without cohesion are most likely formal groups. In these groups, groups at work in particular, the members are often appointed by a superior. This means that the people in the group have to work together with colleagues they possibly don't like. This of course, does not contribute to group cohesion.

In informal groups, the situation is different. Usually in these groups, the members gather voluntarily and without pressure of being appointed.

How can it be, that even informal groups have more or less cohesion within the group?

As mentioned in the previous chapters, the reasons why people in informal groups come together are very different and so are the people. Even in those groups people not necessary like to work together to reach the common aim of the group. But for those people to achieve the common objective is more important, than to work with people they don't like.

As a result of that, informal groups can also be more or less cohesive.

---

[89] Cf. Forsyth (1999), p. 147.

[90] Cf. Black (1951) and Zander (1979) in Luft (1984), p. 18.

14 Results

When we speak of groups in part I of this assignment, social groups are meant.

Groups can be classified in different types. The classification can be done corresponding to different systems.

Group effectiveness is easier to measure in small groups than in big ones. Working groups and teams were implemented with the key-idea of raising the effectiveness of the individual.

Groups, or better the social relationships between human beings have been object of research for many years. The first theories of Lewin made a lot of other scientists research in this field of topic.

In sociology a vast number of studies, researches and dissertations on the topic of groups have been made. We have tried to explain the most common and most used theories.

The topic of informal groups is – in most publications – only a small attachment to the original work. This makes sense, because there is not much difference in the behaviour of the different types of groups.

This assignment has highlighted these differences.

15 Conclusion

Whether formal or informal, groups are part of daily life.

Human beings are confronted with groups in their early life. It could be recorded that group formation begins already in the sandbox, becomes more relevant in kindergarten and in school and is common later during studies, at work and in leisure time.

This may also give reasons for the great and various interests of scientists on this topic.

16 Bibliography

Accel [online]. Productive Workplace – Informal Group Dynamics, http://www.accel-team.com/work_groups/informal_grps_02.html (2 von 2) [Accessed 09 May 2009]

Ammon, G. (1976): Analytische Gruppendynamik, Hamburg: Hoffmann und Campe Verlag.

Anderman, U. and Drees, M. and Grätz, F. (2006): Wie verfasst man wissenschaftliche Arbeiten?, Mannheim: Bibliographisches Institut & F. A. Brockhaus AG

Antons, K. (1996): Praxis der Gruppendynamik, 6th edition, Göttingen: Hogrefe-Verlag

Antons, K. and Aman, A. and Clausen, G. (2004):Gruppenprozesse verstehen, 2nd edition, Wiesbaden: VS Verlag für Sozialwissenschaften

Arnscheid, R. (1999): Gemeinsam sind wir stark? Zum Zusammenhang zwischen Gruppenkohäsion und Gruppenleistung, Münster: Waxmann Verlag GmbH.

Barker, L., L./Wahlers, K., J./Cegala, D., J./Kibler, R. J. (1983): Groups In Process, An Introduction to Small Group Communication, New Yersey: Prentice-Hall, Inc.

Battegay, R. (1974): Der Mensch in der Gruppe, Bern/Stuttgart/Wien: Verlag Hans Huber

Bernstein, S./Lowy, L. (1969): Untersuchungen zur Sozialen Gruppenarbeit in Theorie und Praxis, Freiburg im Breisgau: Lambertus-Verlag.

Bernstein, S./Lowy, L. (1978): Neue Untersuchungen zur Sozialen Gruppenarbeit, 2nd edition, Freiburg im Breisgau: Lambertus-Verlag.

Blair, G. [online]. Groups that Work, http://www.see.ed.ac.uk/~gerard/Management/a...www.ee.ed.ac.uk/~gerard/Management/art0.html [Accessed 09 May 2009], University of Edinburgh

Brown, R. (1988): Group Processes, Dynamics within and between Groups, Oxford/New York: Basil Blackwell Ltd.

Claessens, D. (1995): Gruppe und Gruppenverbände, 2nd edition, Hamburg: Verlag Dr. Kovač

Clinchy, E., R. (1952): Handbuch für Menschliche Beziehungen, Bad Nauheim: Christian-Verlag.

Däumling, A./Fengler, J./Nellessen, L./Svensson, A. (1974): Angewandte Gruppendynamik, Selbsterfahrung, Forschungsergebnisse, Trainingsmodelle, Stuttgart: Ernst Klett Verlag.

Deutsches Institut für Wirtschaftsforschung [online]. Frauen in Führungspositionen verdienen rund ein Viertel weniger als Männer, http://www.diw.de/deutsch/pressemitteilungen/432.html?language=de [Accessed 01 June 2009]

Edding, C. and Schattenhofer K., (2009): Handbuch Alles über Gruppen: Theorie, Anwendung, Praxis, Weinheim and Basel: Beltz Verlag.

Festinger, L./Schachter, S./Back, K. (1959): Social Pressure in Informal Groups, London: Tavistock Publications

Forsyth, D. (1999): Group Dynamics, 3rd edition, Belmont: Wadsworth Publishing Company

Frese, E. (2005): Grundlagen der Organisation, 9th edition, Wiesbaden: Betriebswirtschaftlicher Verlag Dr. Th. Gabler/GWV Fachverlag GmbH.

Gahagan, J. (1975): Interpersonal and Group Behaviour, London: Methuen & Co Ltd.

Gairing, F. (2002): Organisationsentwicklung als Lernprozess von Menschen und System, 3rd edition, Weinheim and Basel: Beltz Verlag

Gellert, M. and Nowak, K. (2004): Teamarbeit – Teamentwicklung – Teamberatung. Ein Praxisbuch für die Arbeit in und mit Teams. Meezen: Limmer.

Hofstätter, P. (1993): Gruppendynamik, 3rd edition, Reinbek bei Hamburg: Rowohlt Taschenbuch Verlag GmbH

Homans, G., C. (1978): Theorie der sozialen Gruppe, 7th edition, Opladen: Westdeutscher Verlag.

Kidder, L./Stewart, V. (1975): The Psychology of Intergroup Relations – Conflict and Consciousness

König, O. (editor) (2001): Gruppendynamik, 6th edition, München: Profil Verlag GmbH

König, O./Schattenhofer, K. (2006): Einführung in die Gruppendynamik, Heidelberg: Carl-Auer-Systeme.

Kretschmar, A. (1994): Angewandte Soziologie im Unternehmen, Wiesbaden: Gabler.

Langmaack B. and Braune-Krickau, M. (2000):Wie die Gruppe laufen lernt: Anregungen zum Planen und Leiten von Gruppen. Ein praktisches Lehrbuch, 7th edition, Weinheim: Beltz-Verlag.

Leber, A./Trescher, H.-G./Büttner, Ch. (1985a): Die Bedeutung der Gruppe für die Sozialisation, Teil I, Kindheit und Familie, Göttingen: Verlag für Medizinische Psychologie.

Leber, A./Trescher, H.-G./Büttner, Ch. (1985b): Die Bedeutung der Gruppe für die Sozialisation, Teil II, Beruf und Gesellschaft, Göttingen: Verlag für Medizinische Psychologie.

Lechner, H. (2001): Die Erklärung von Gruppenprozessen, Systematisierung und Vergleich anhand formaler Modelle, Frankfurt am Main: Peter Lang, Europäischer Verlag der Wissenschaften.

Long, S. (1992): A Structural Analysis of Small Groups, London/New York: Routledge.

Luft, J. (1984): Group Processes – An Introduction to Group Dynamics, 3rd edition, Paolo Alto: Mayfield Publishing Company

Lutz, A. (2005): Praxisbuch Networking, Wien: Linde Verlag.

Mann, L. (1999): Sozialpsychologie, Weinheim und Basel: Beltz Verlag.

Mills, Th., M. (1976): Soziologie der Gruppe, Band 10, 5th edition, München: Juventa Verlag.

Nikles, B. W. (2008): Institutionen und Organisationen der Sozialen Arbeit, Stuttgart: Uni-Taschenbücher GmbH.

Reeves, E., T. (1970): Dynamics of Group Behaviour, New York: American Management Association, Inc.

Sader, M. (1988): Psychologie der Gruppe, 6th edition, Weinheim/München: Juventa Verlag.

Runde, A. and Warmbrunn, A. (2006): In Gruppen und Teams zusammenarbeiten, München: Urban & Fischer Verlag.

Schauf, M. (2009): Scrip for the FOM MBA-Module „Soft skills & Leadership Qualities"

Schreyögg, G. (2003): Organisation: Grundlagen moderner Organisationsgestaltung. Mit Fallstudien, 4th edition, Wiesbaden: Gabler.

Seliger, R. (2008): Einführung in Großgruppenmethoden, Heidelberg: Carl-Auer-Systeme Verlag.

Stahl, E. (2002): Dynamik in Gruppen, Handbuch der Gruppenleitung, Weinheim, Basel , Berlin: Verlagsgruppe Beltz.

Stahl, E. (2007): Dynamik in Gruppen, 2nd edition, Weinheim: Beltz Verlag

Trappmann, M., Hummell, H. J. and W. Sodeur (2005): Strukturanalyse sozialer Netzwerke, Konzepte, Modelle, Mothoden, Wiesbaden: VS Verlag für Sozialwissenschaften/GWV Fachverlage GmbH.

Vorwerg, M. (1969): Sozialpsychologische Optimierung von Gruppenleistungen, Jena: Friedrich-Schiller-Universität.

Zulliger, H. (1961): Horde-Bande-Gemeinschaft, Stuttgart: Ernst Klett Verlag